Enjoy!!!

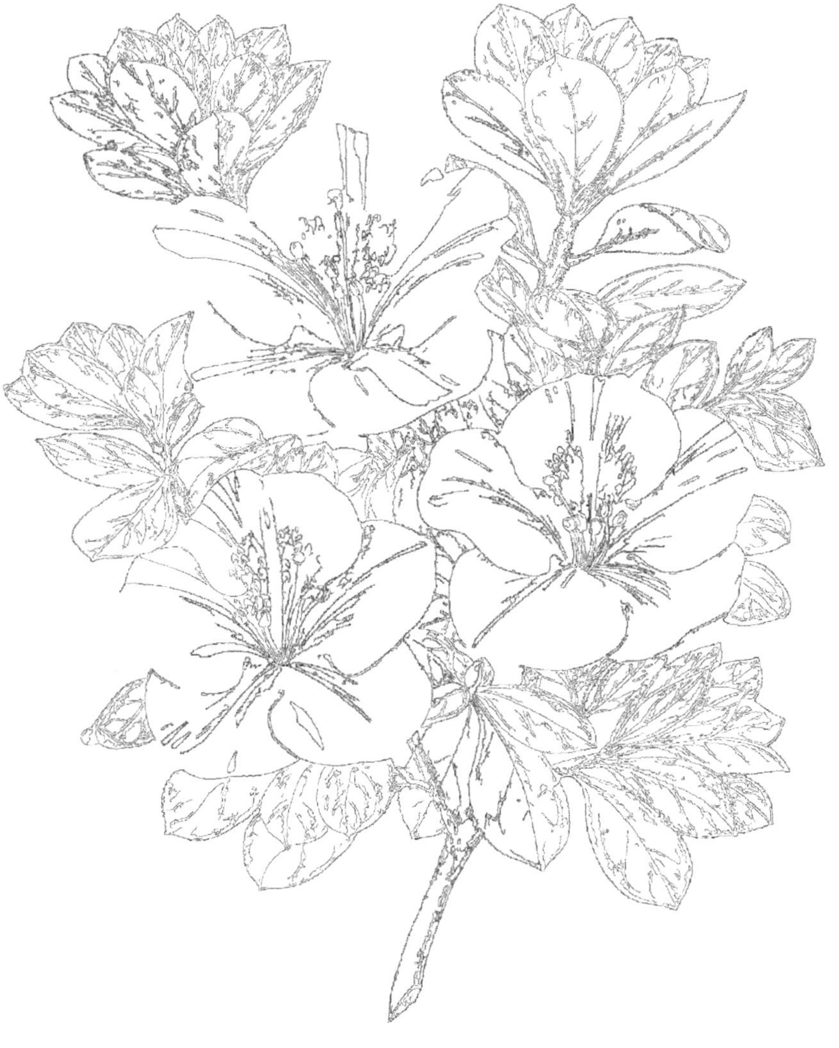

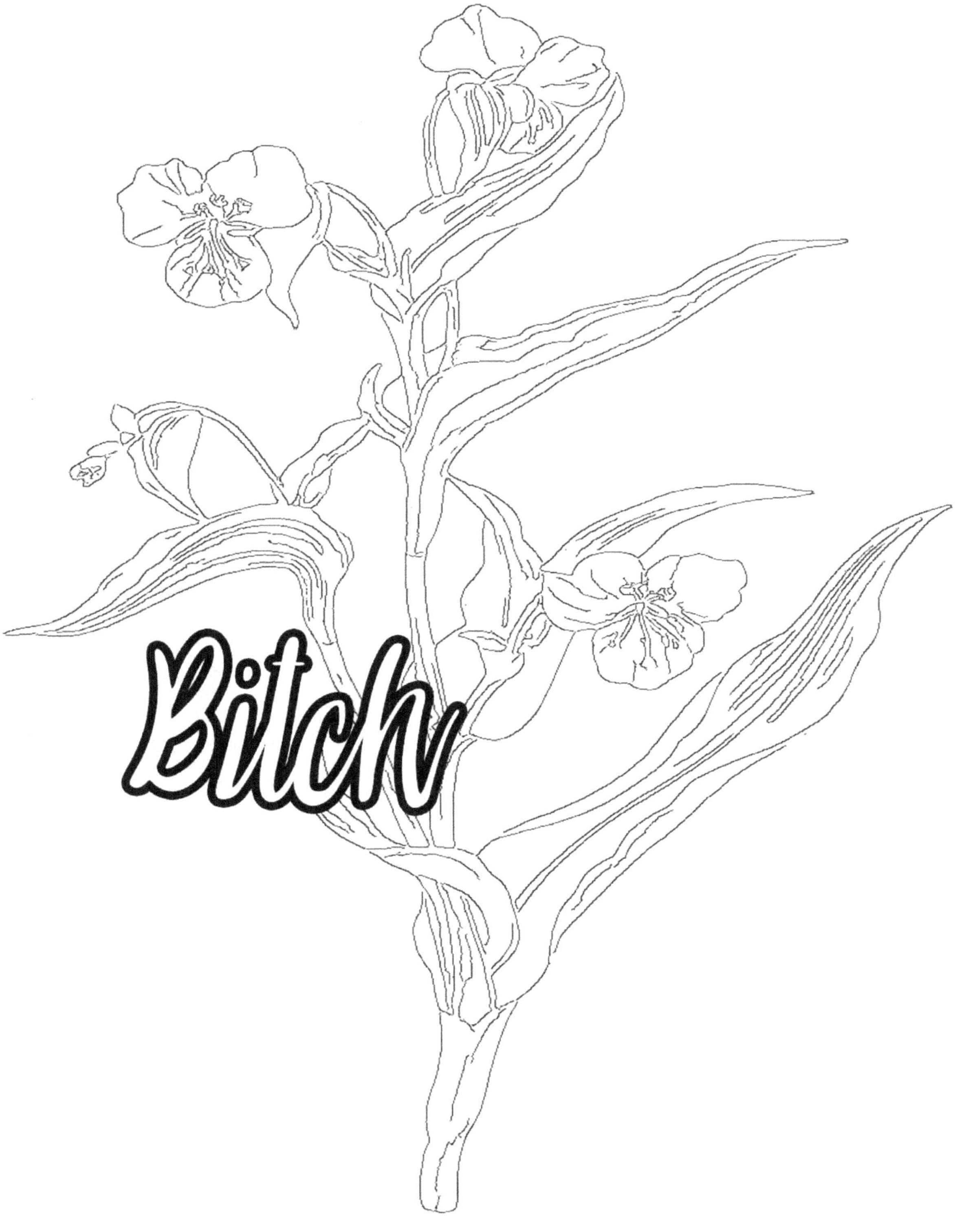
Bitch

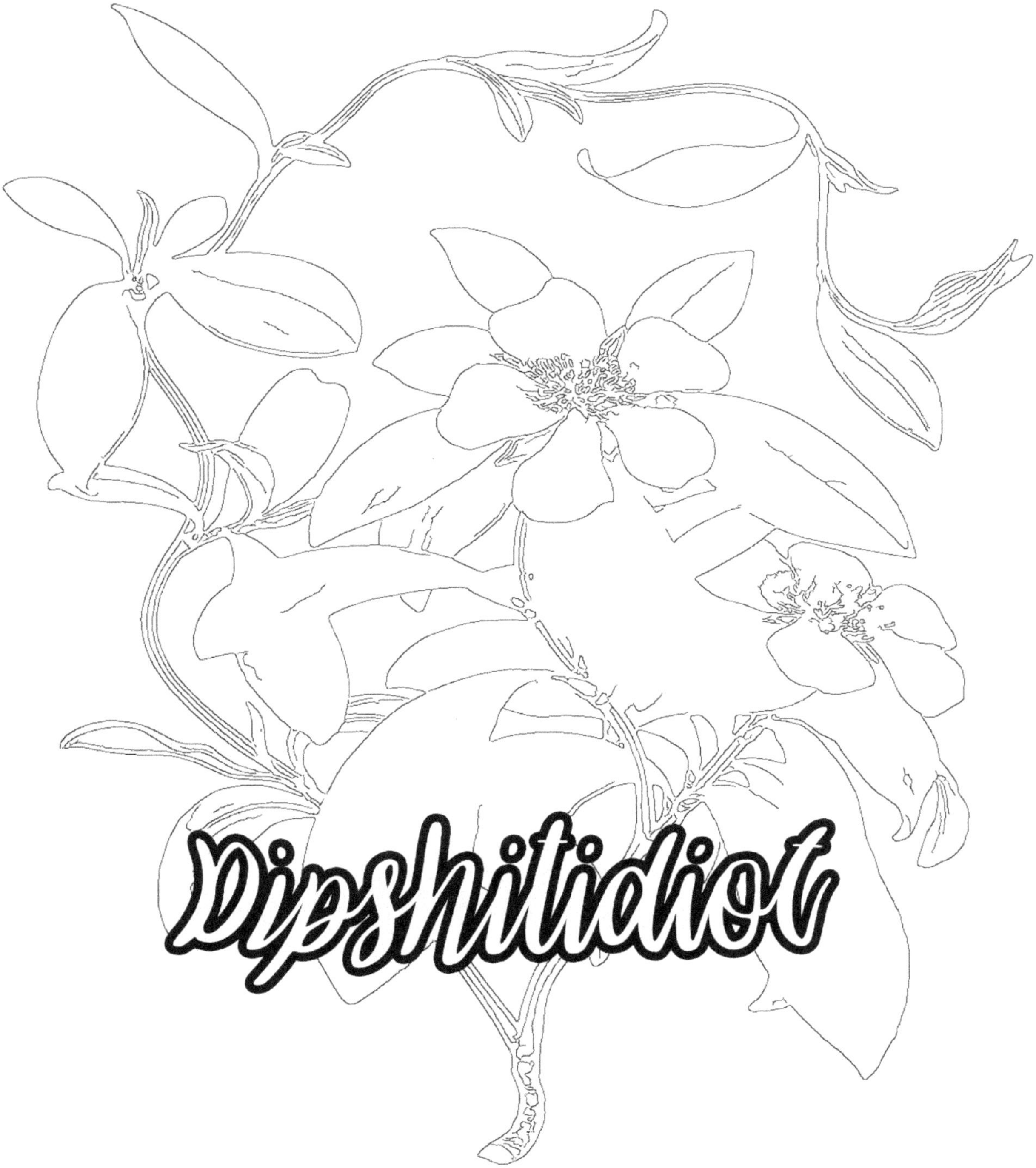
Dipshitidiot

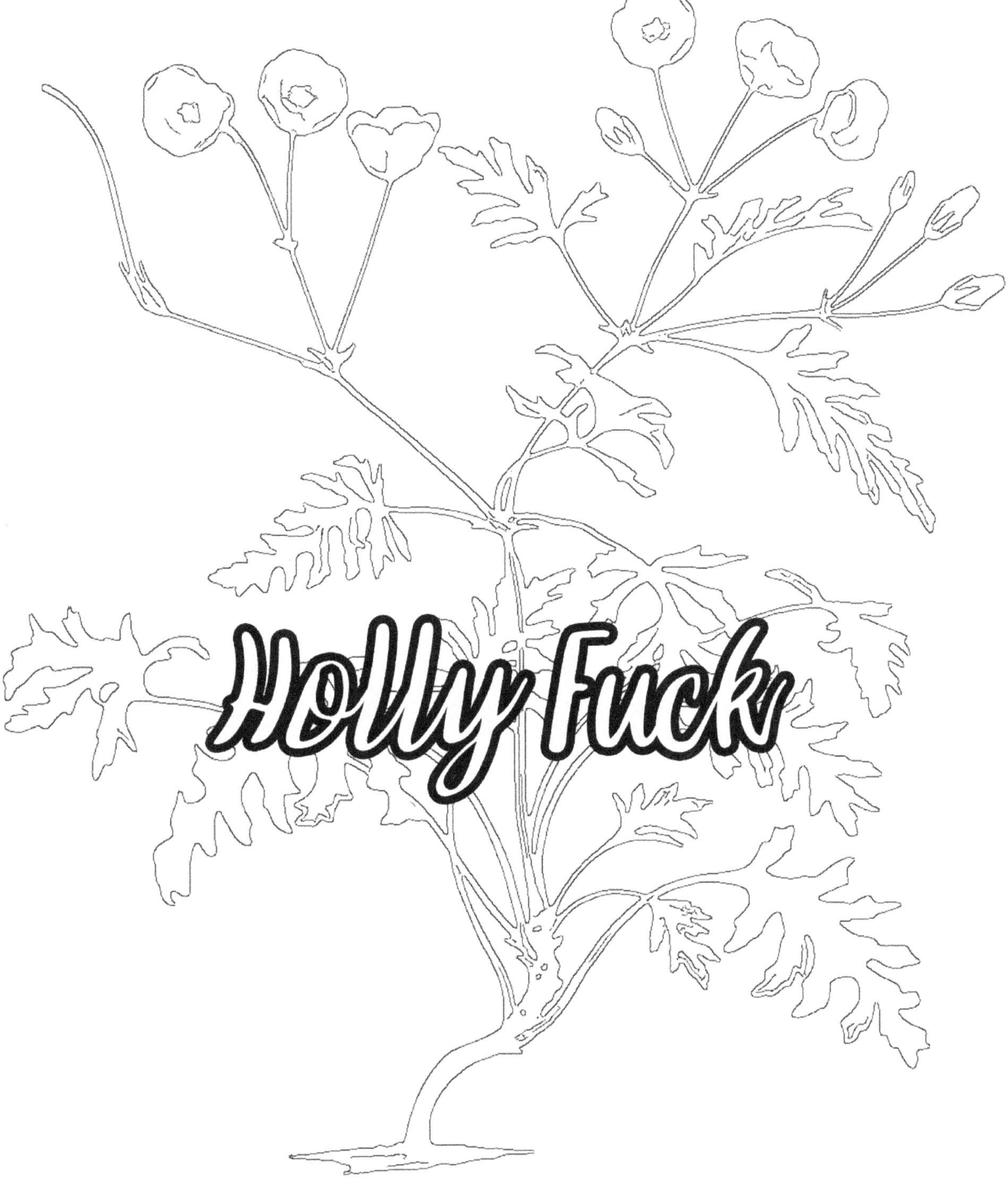
Holly Fuck

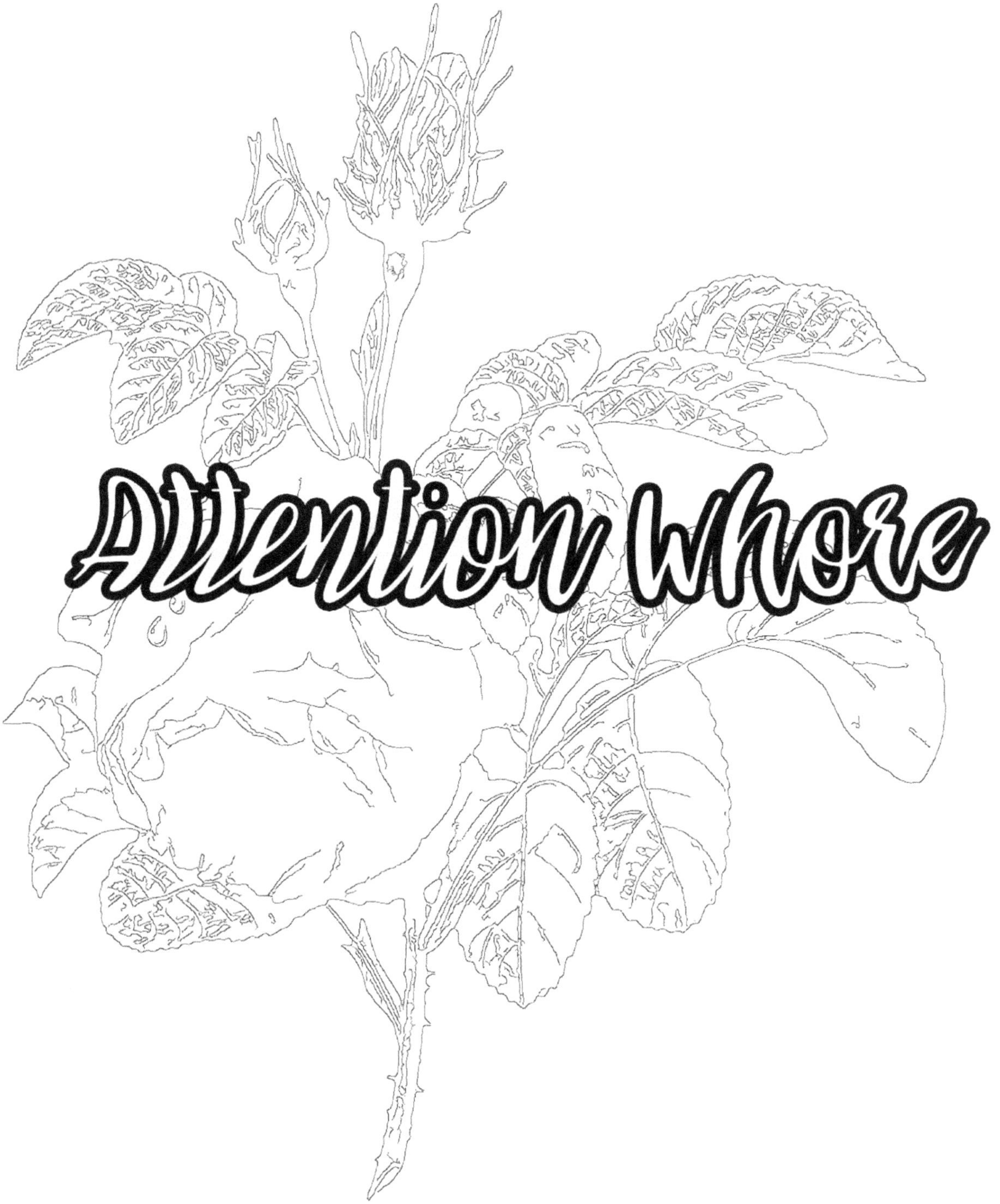
Attention Whore

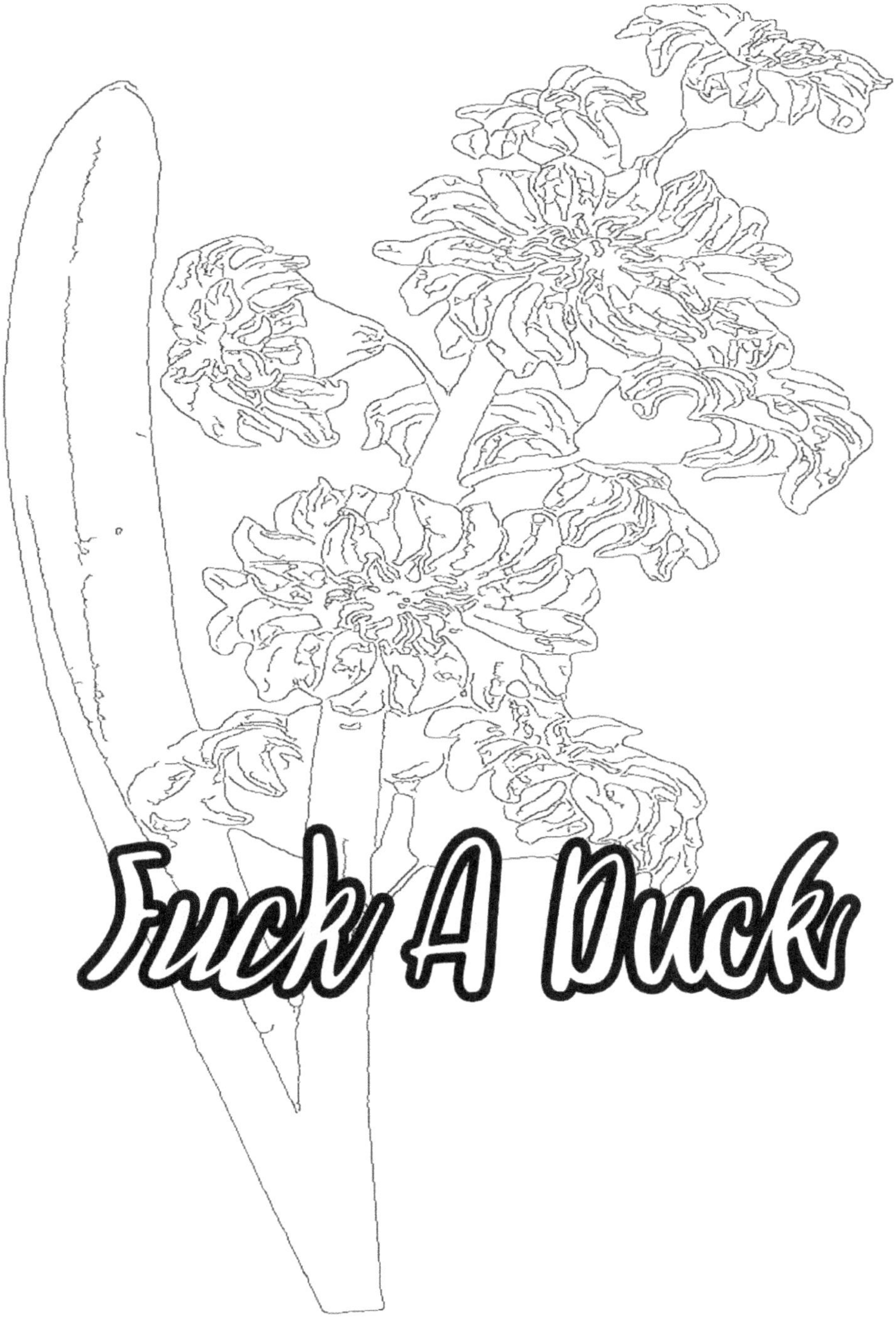
Fuck A Duck

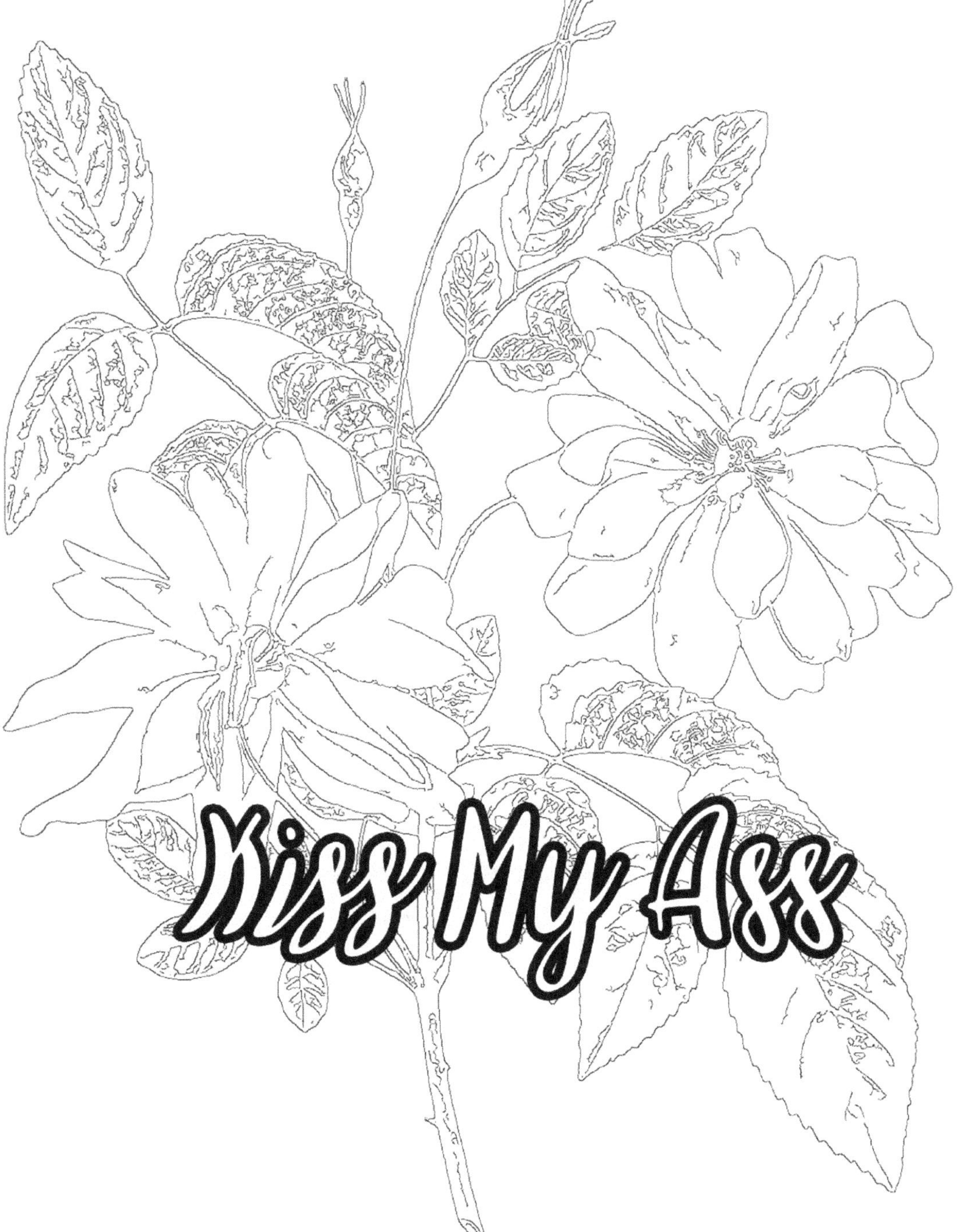
Kiss My Ass

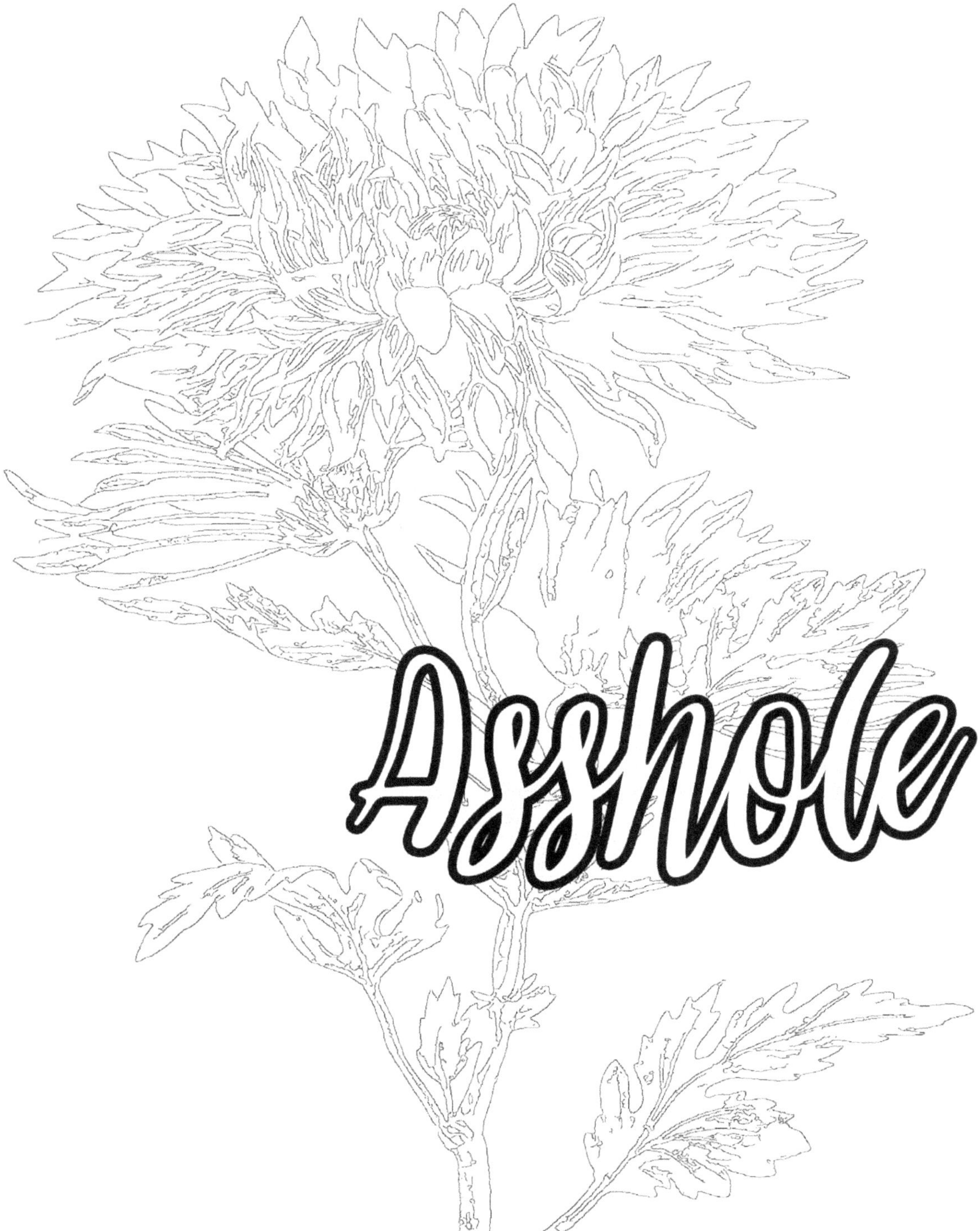
Asshole

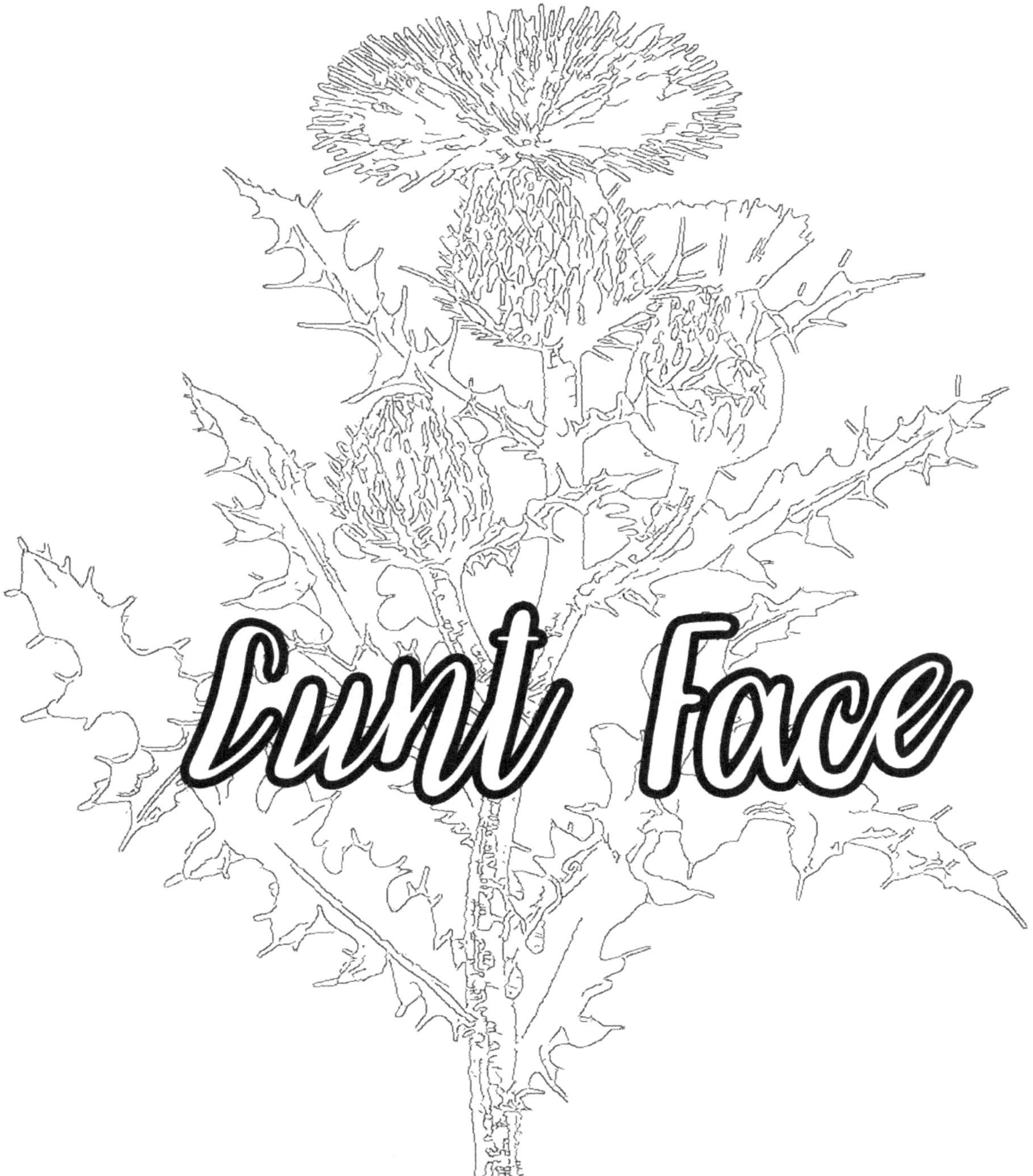
Cunt Face

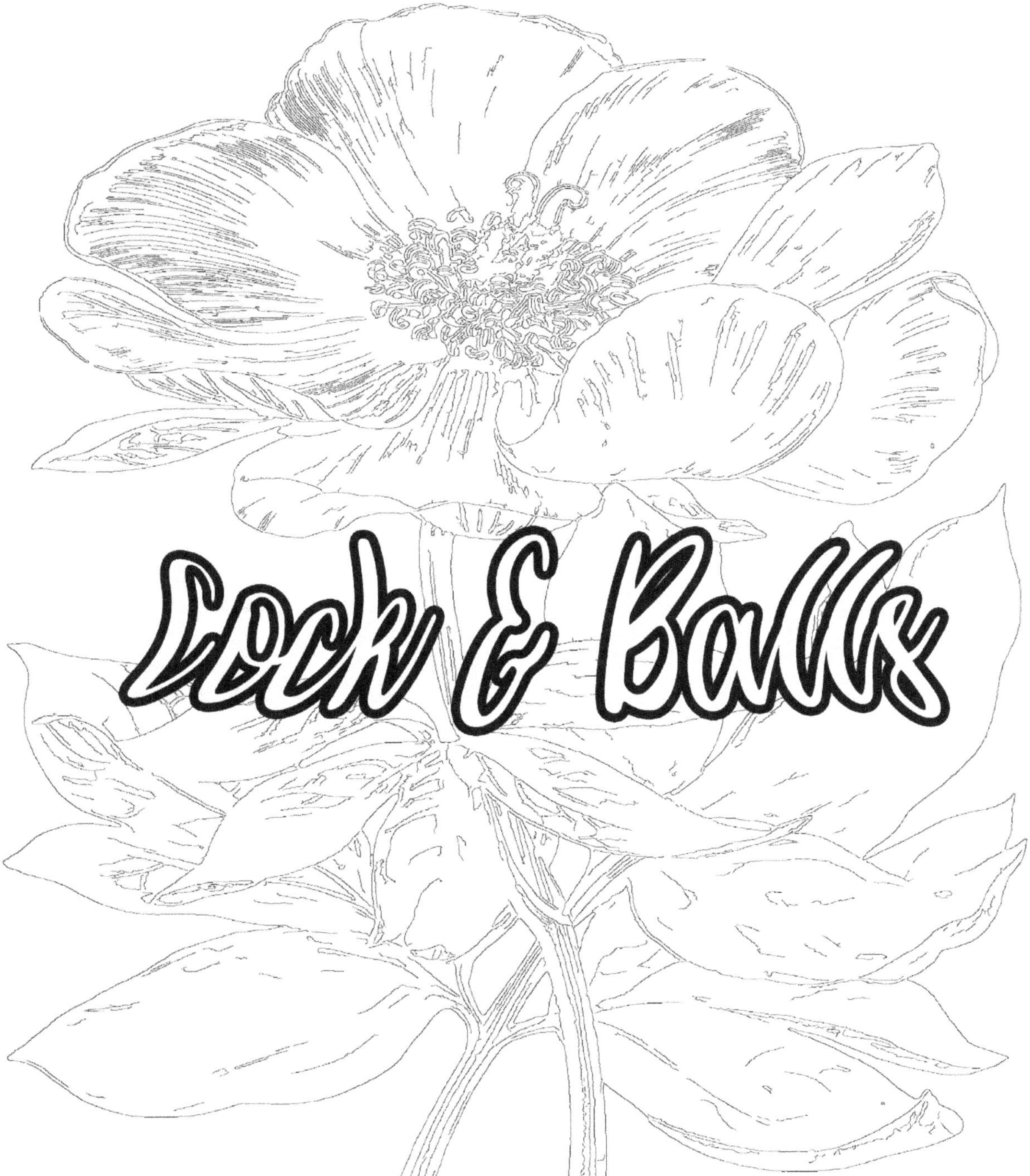
Cock & Balls

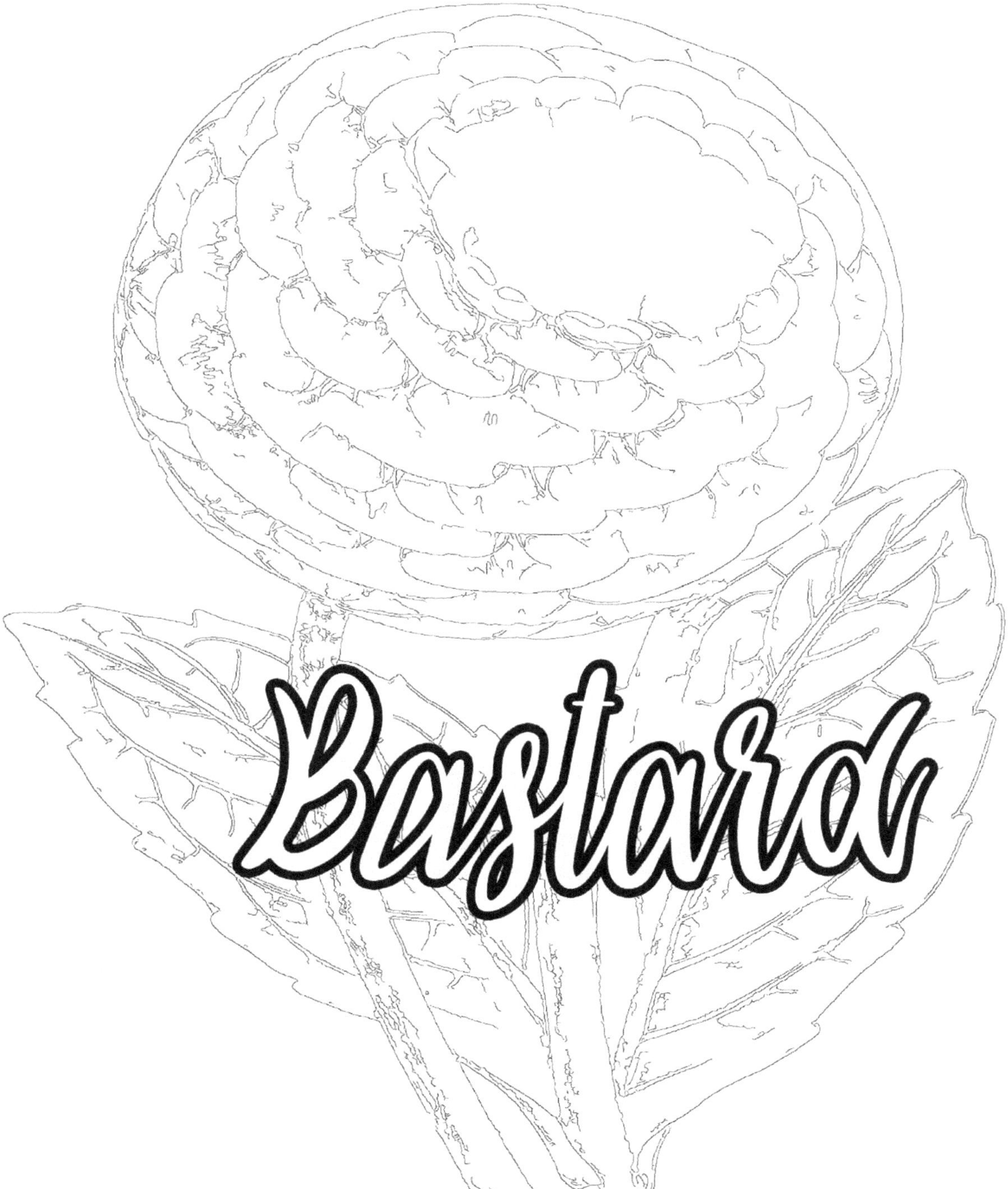
Bastard

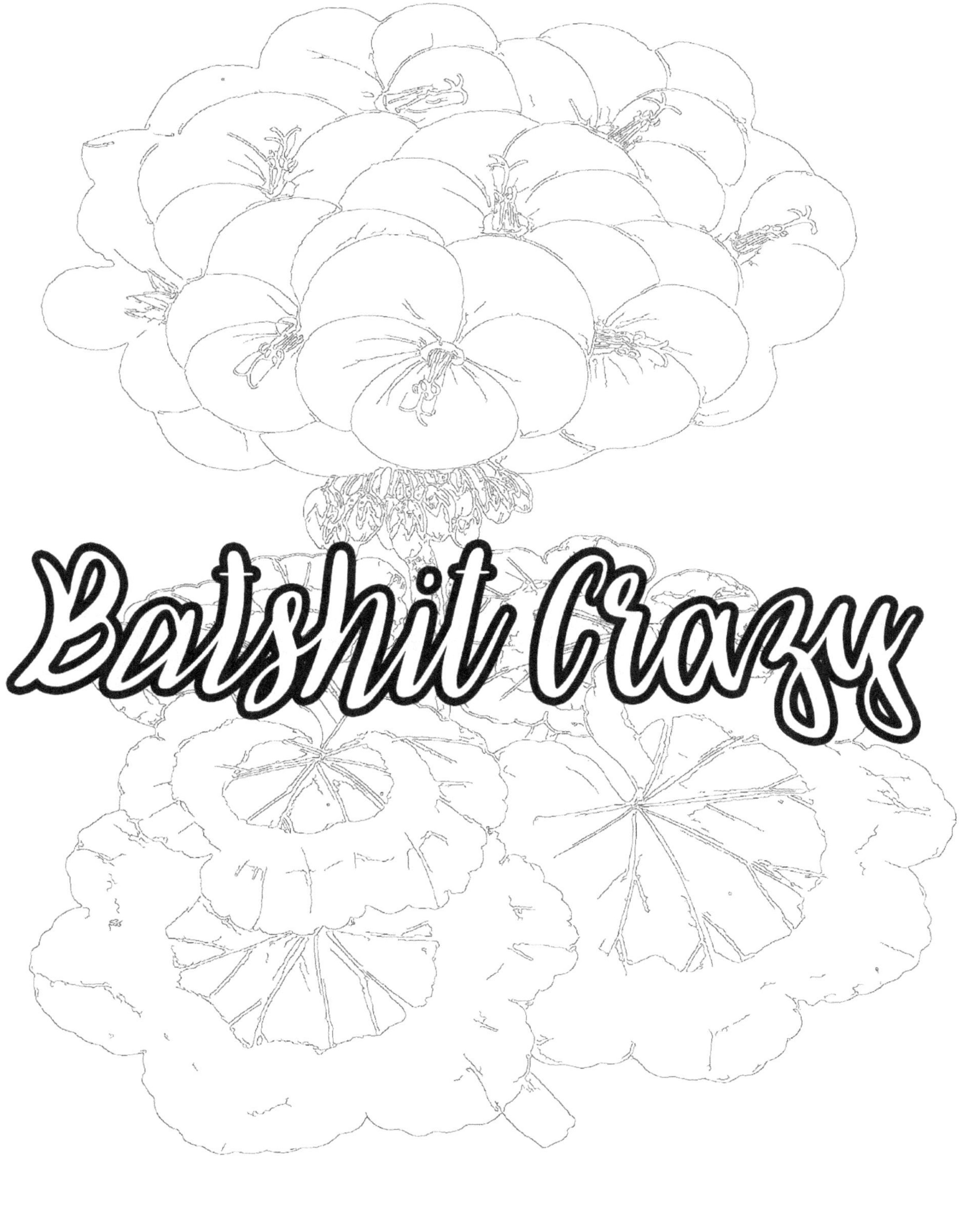
Batshit Crazy

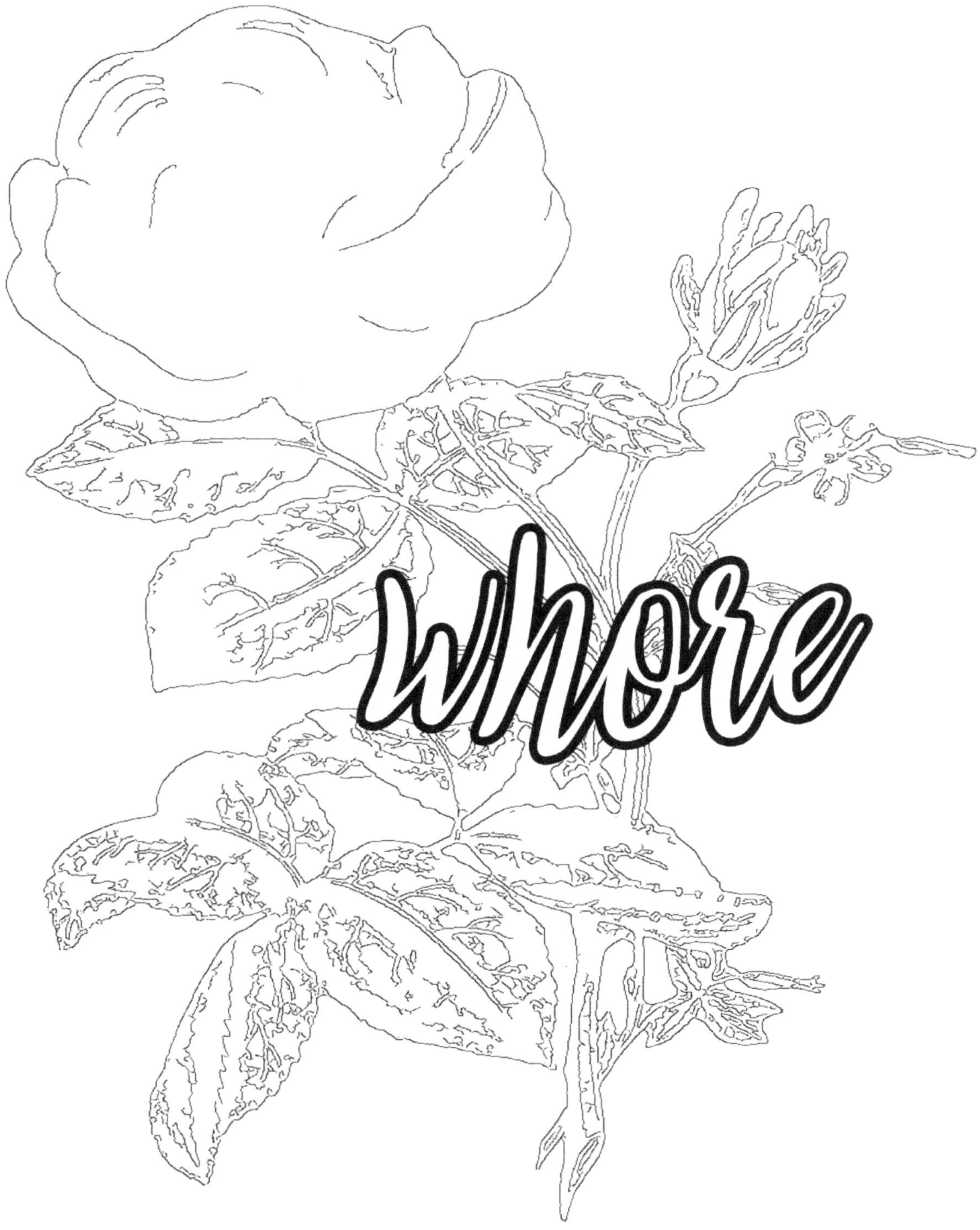
whore

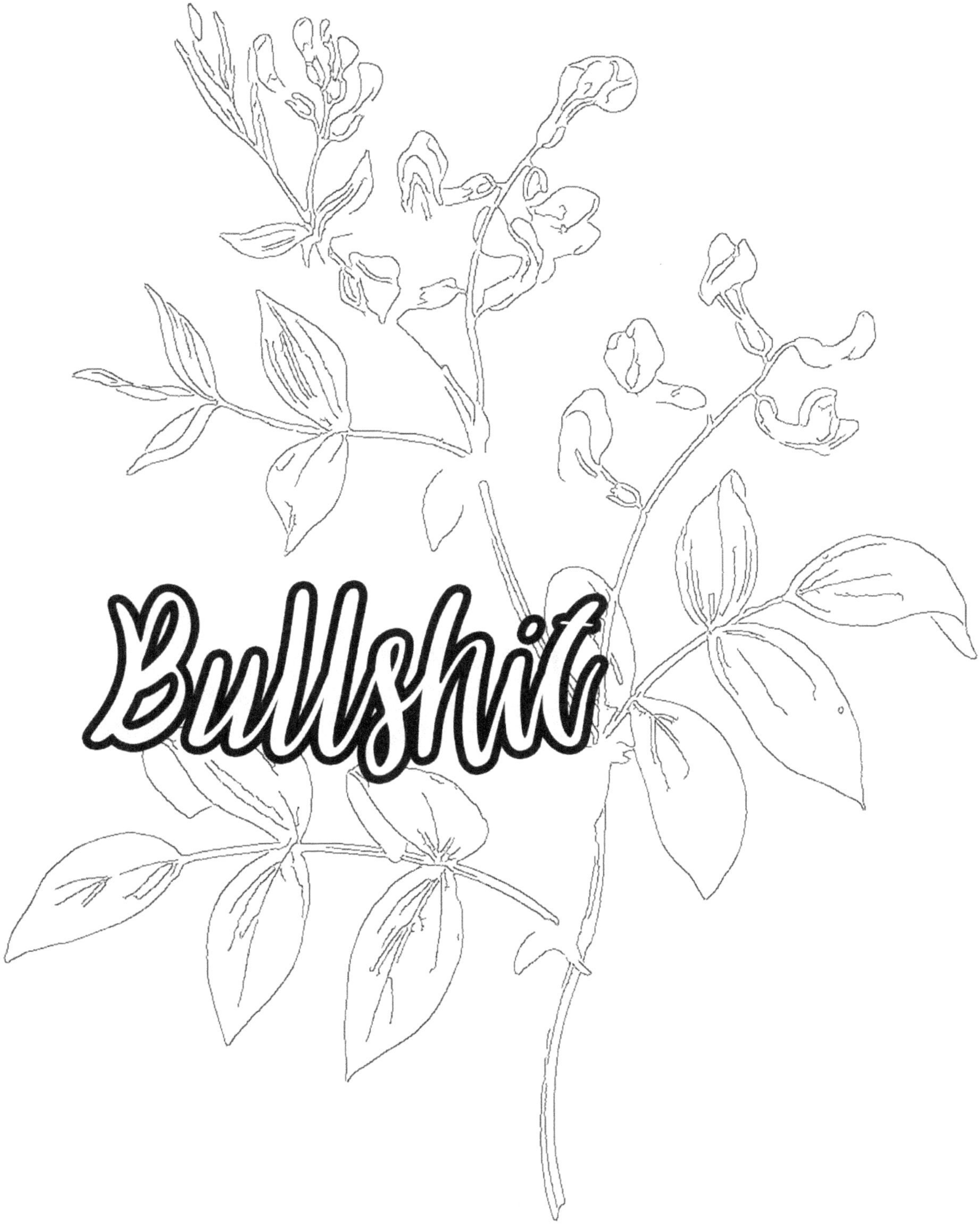
Bullshit

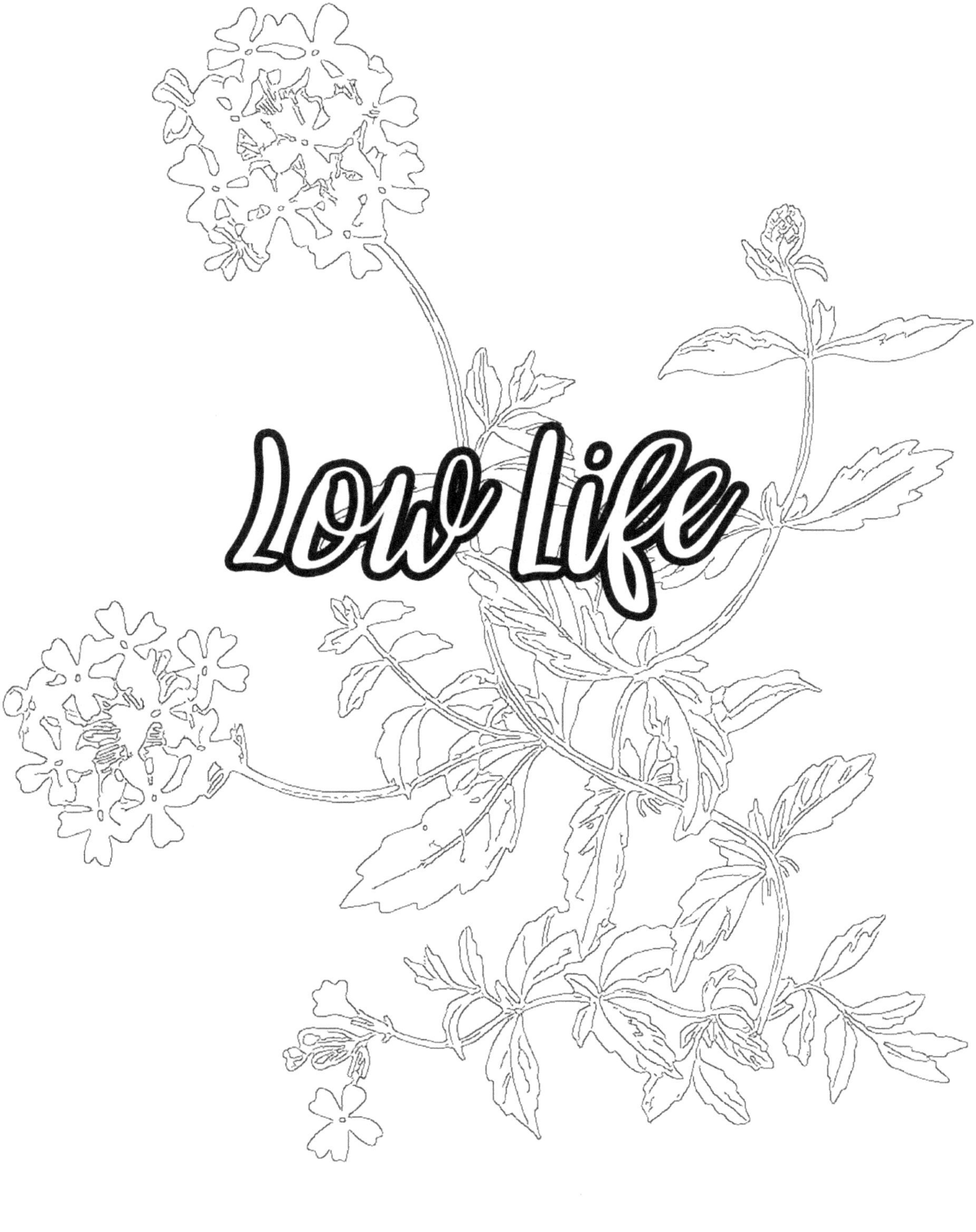
Low Life

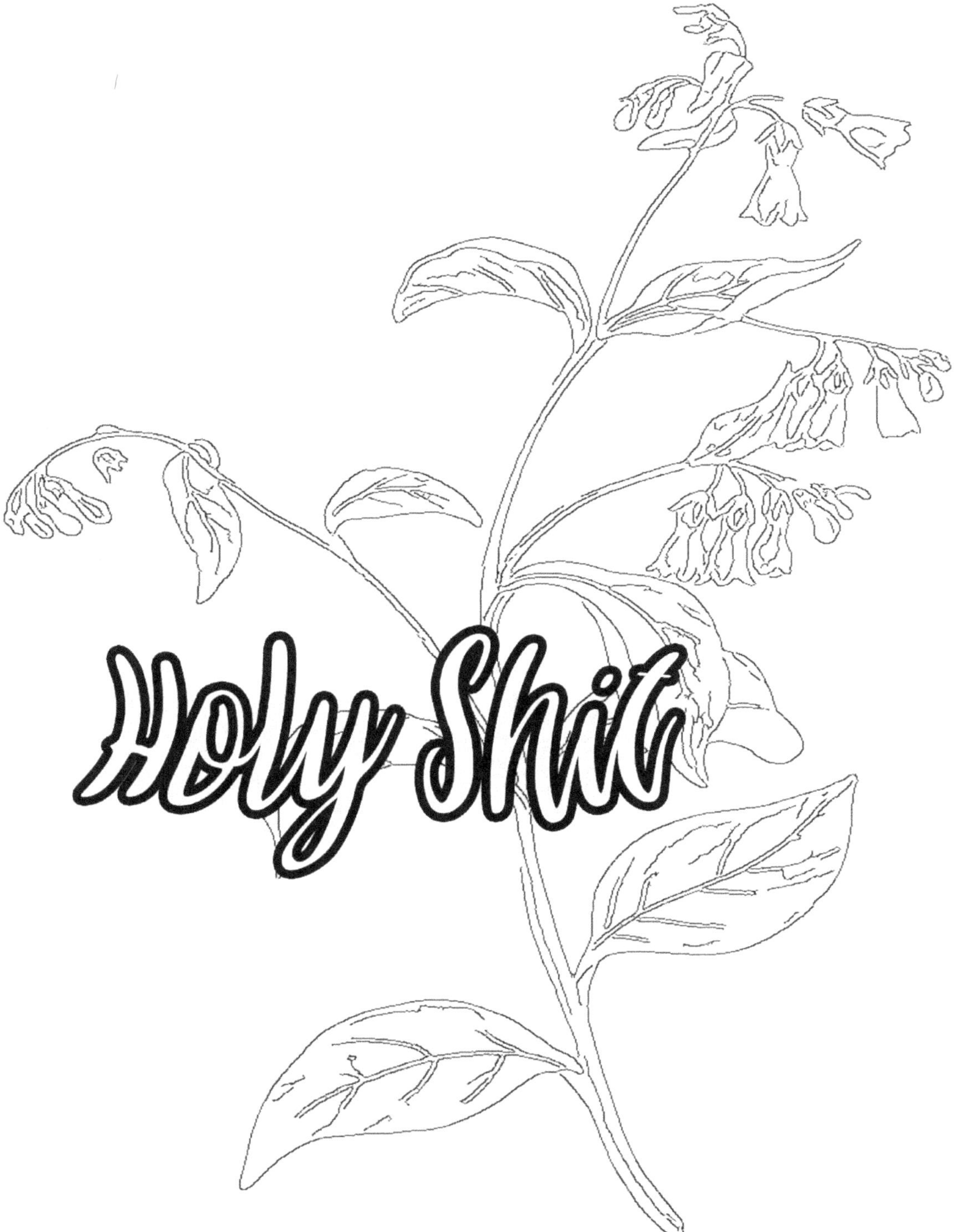
Holy Shit

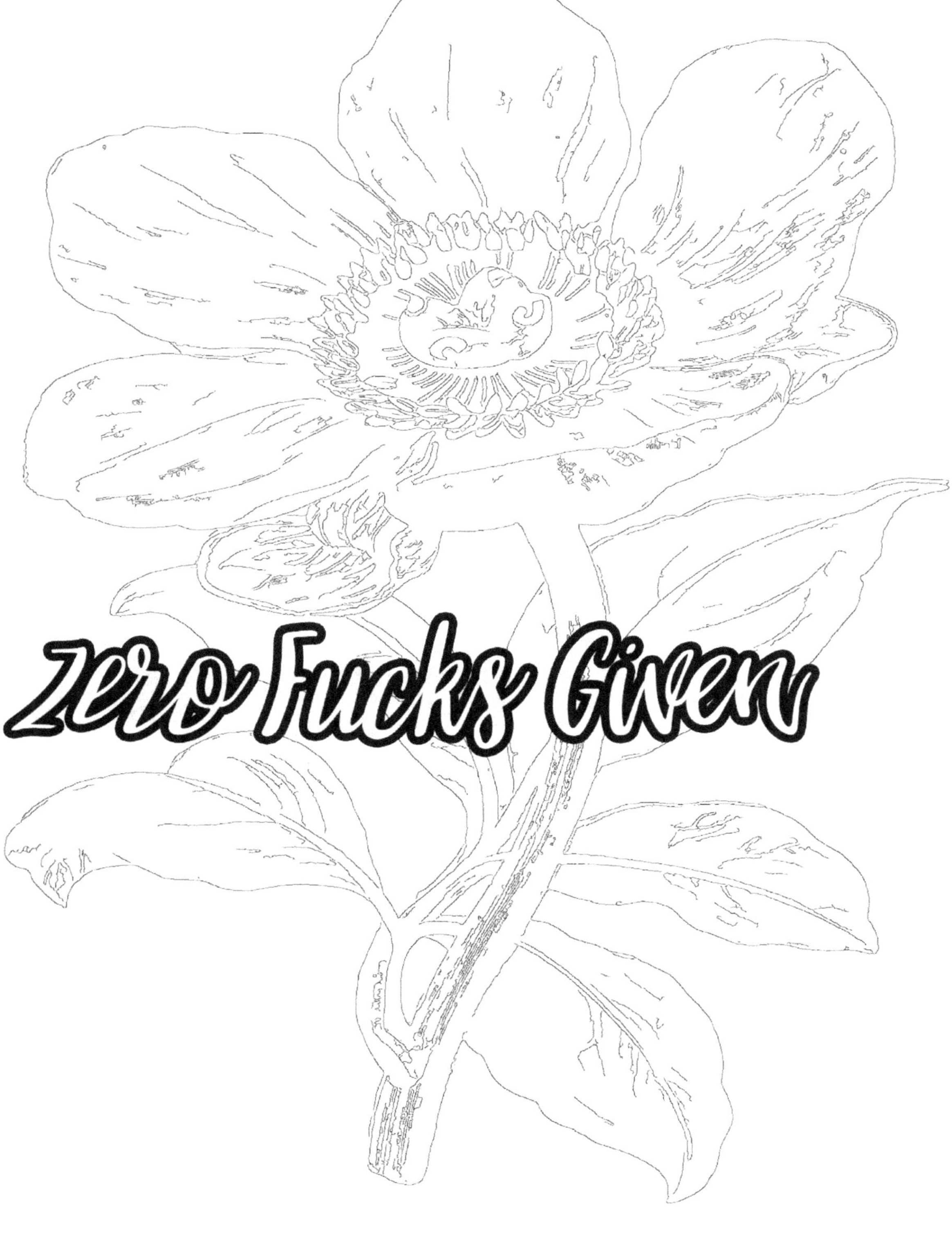
Zero Fucks Given

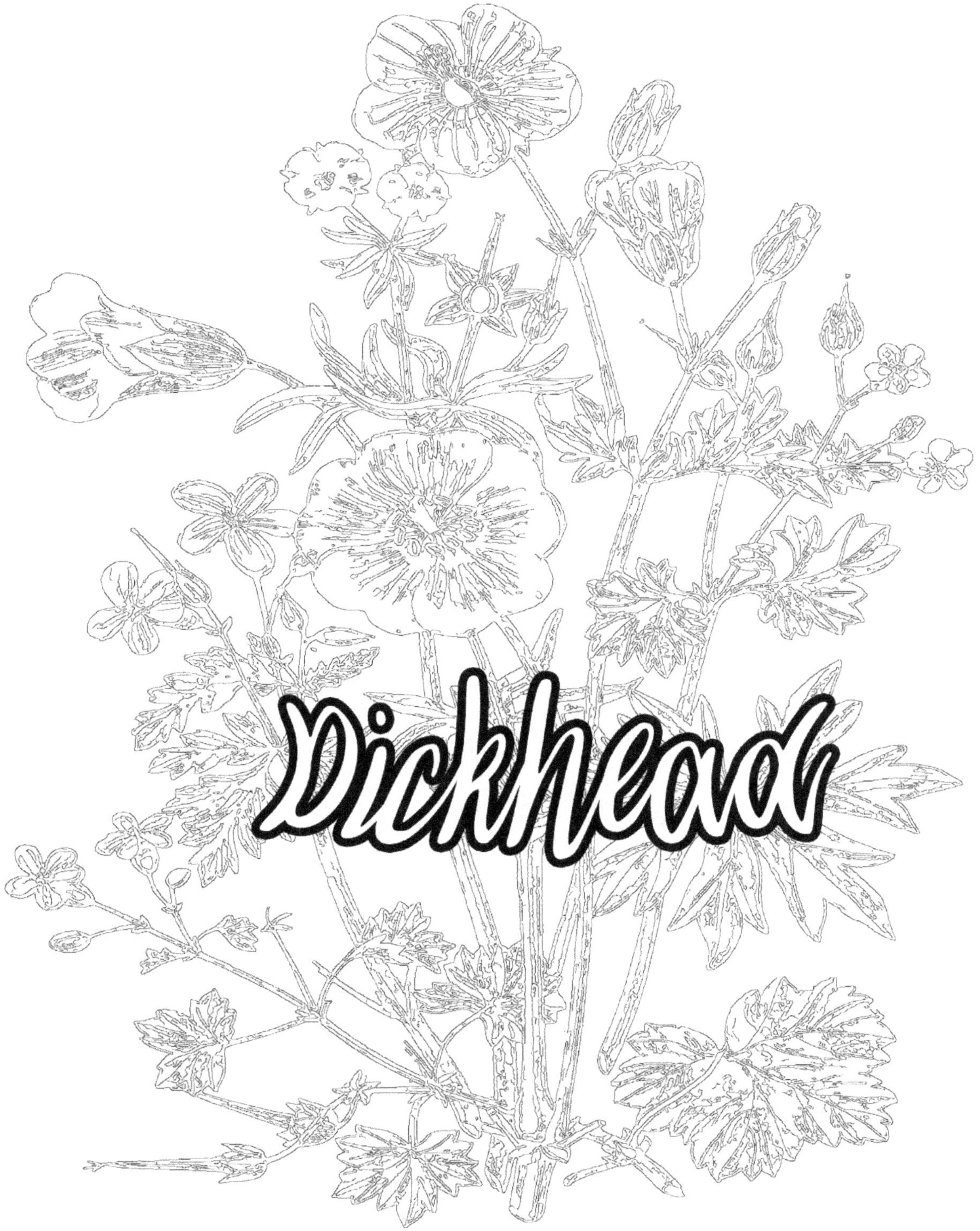
Dickhead

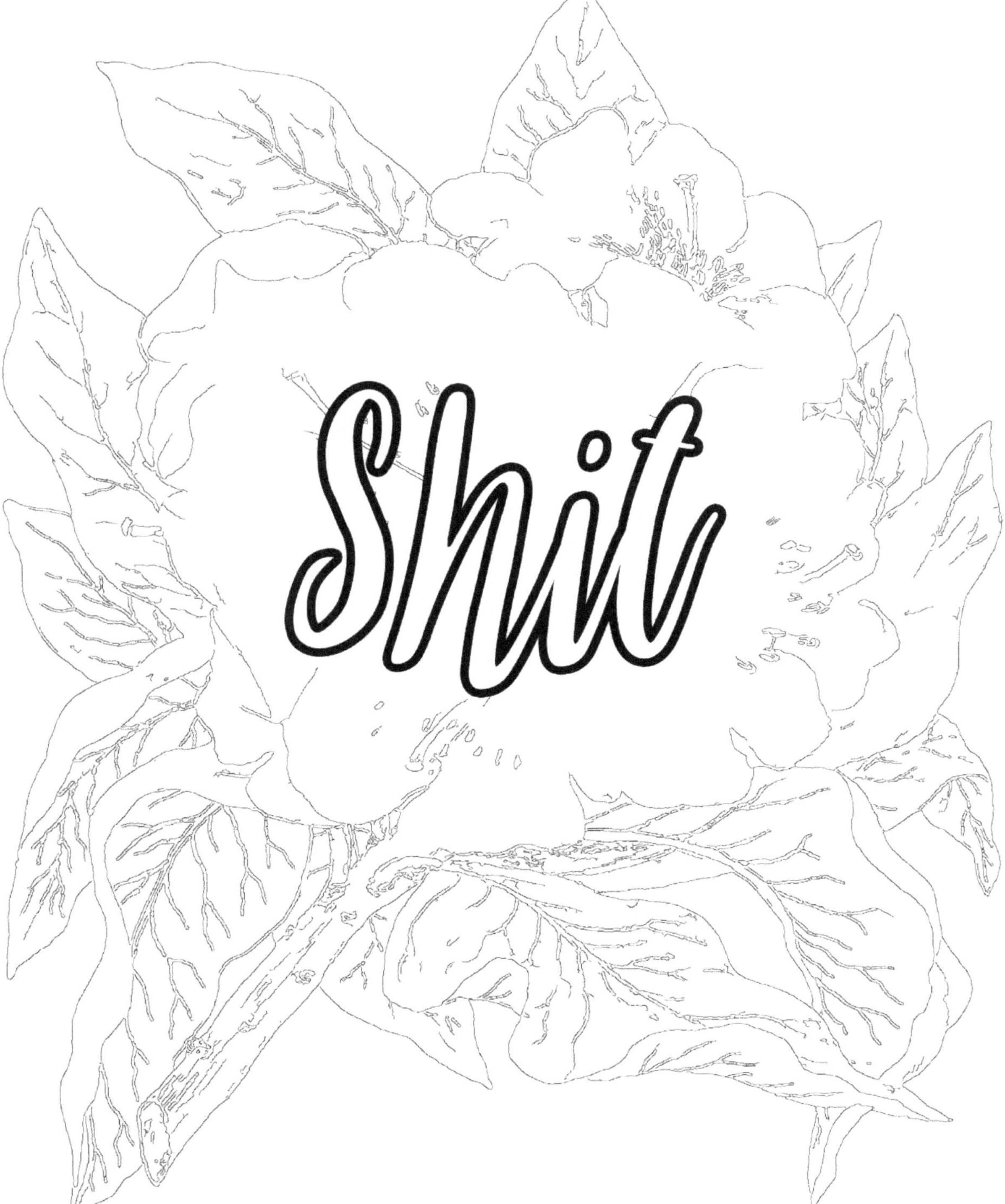
Shit

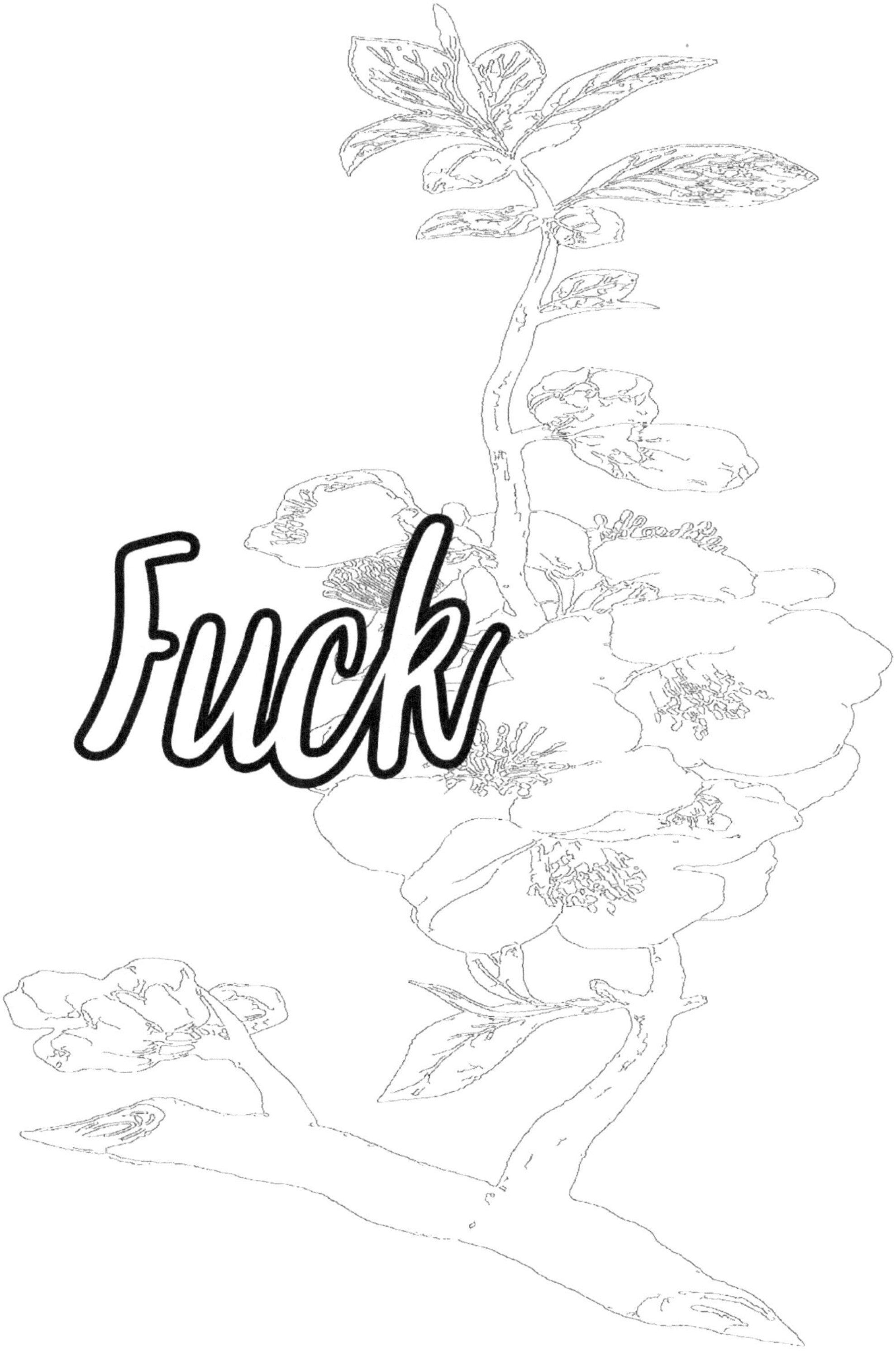
Fuck

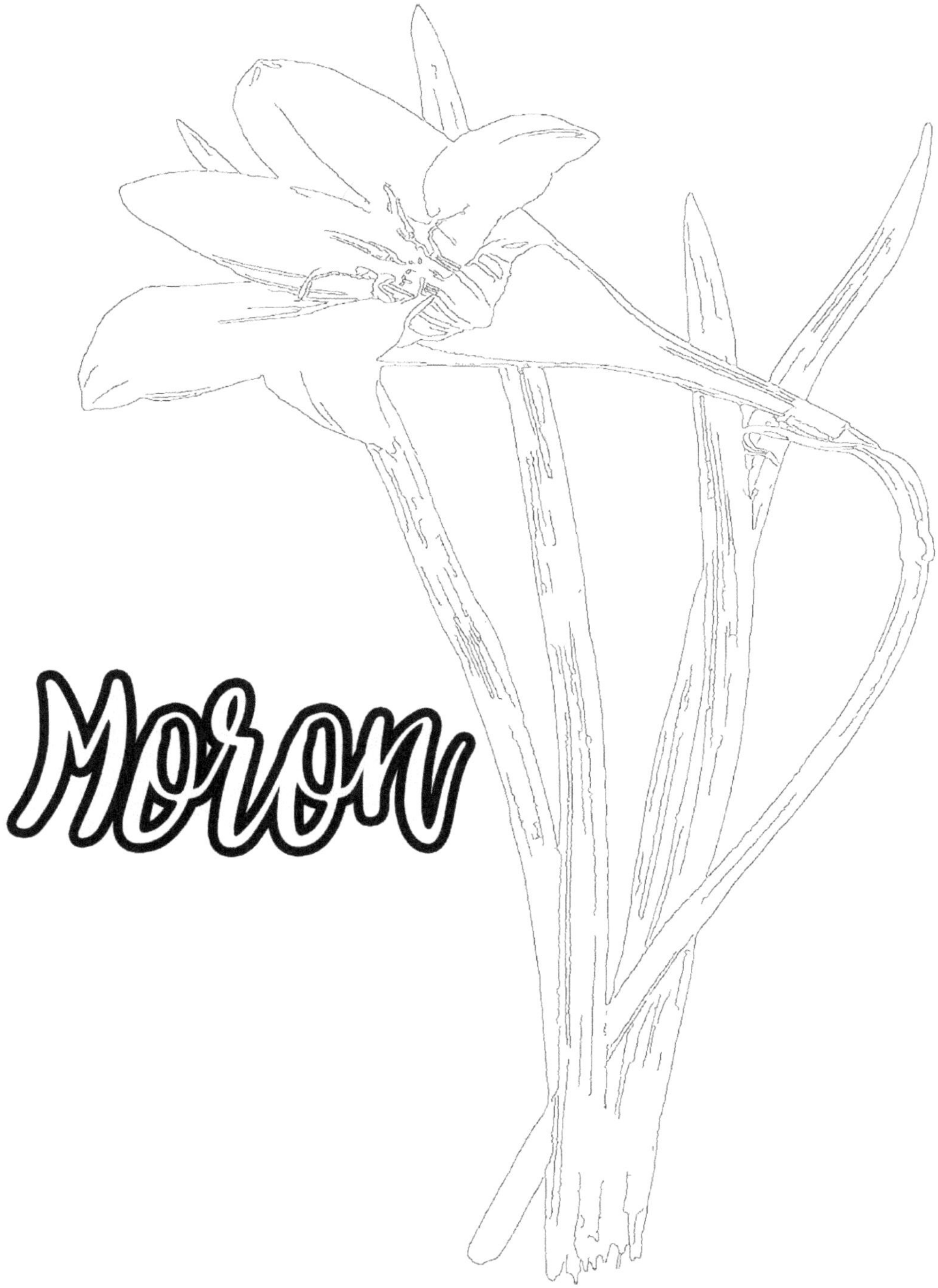
Moron

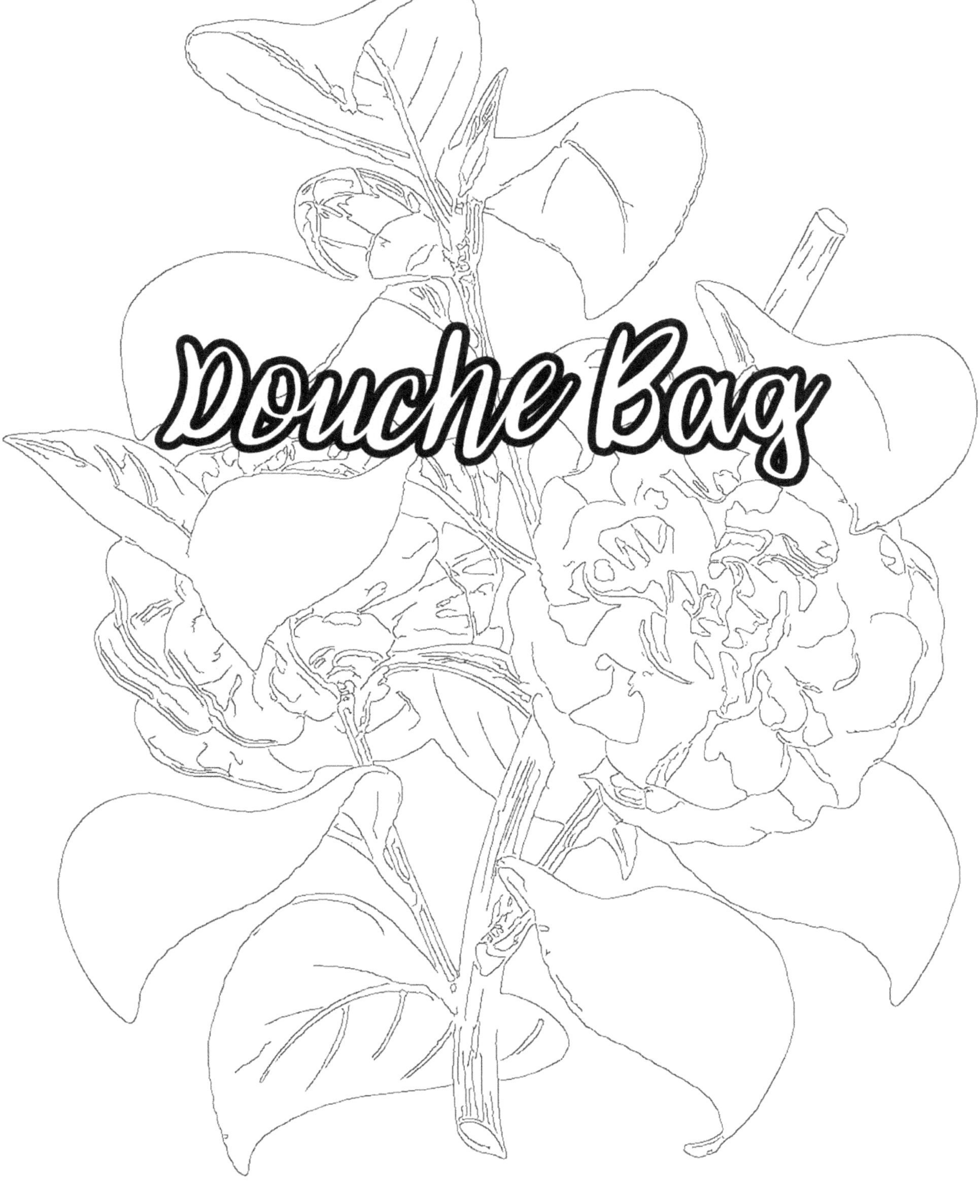
Douche Bag

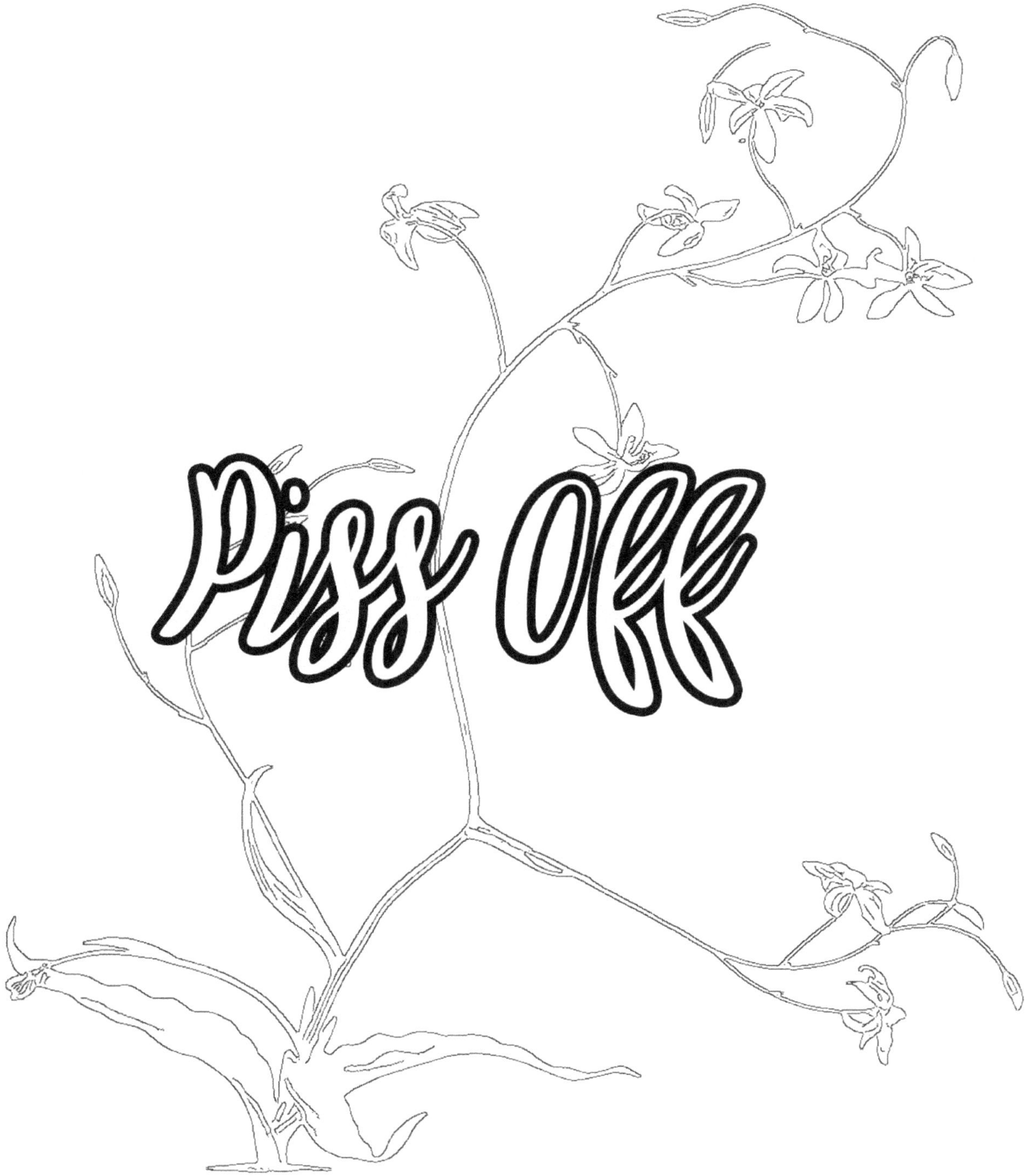
Piss Off

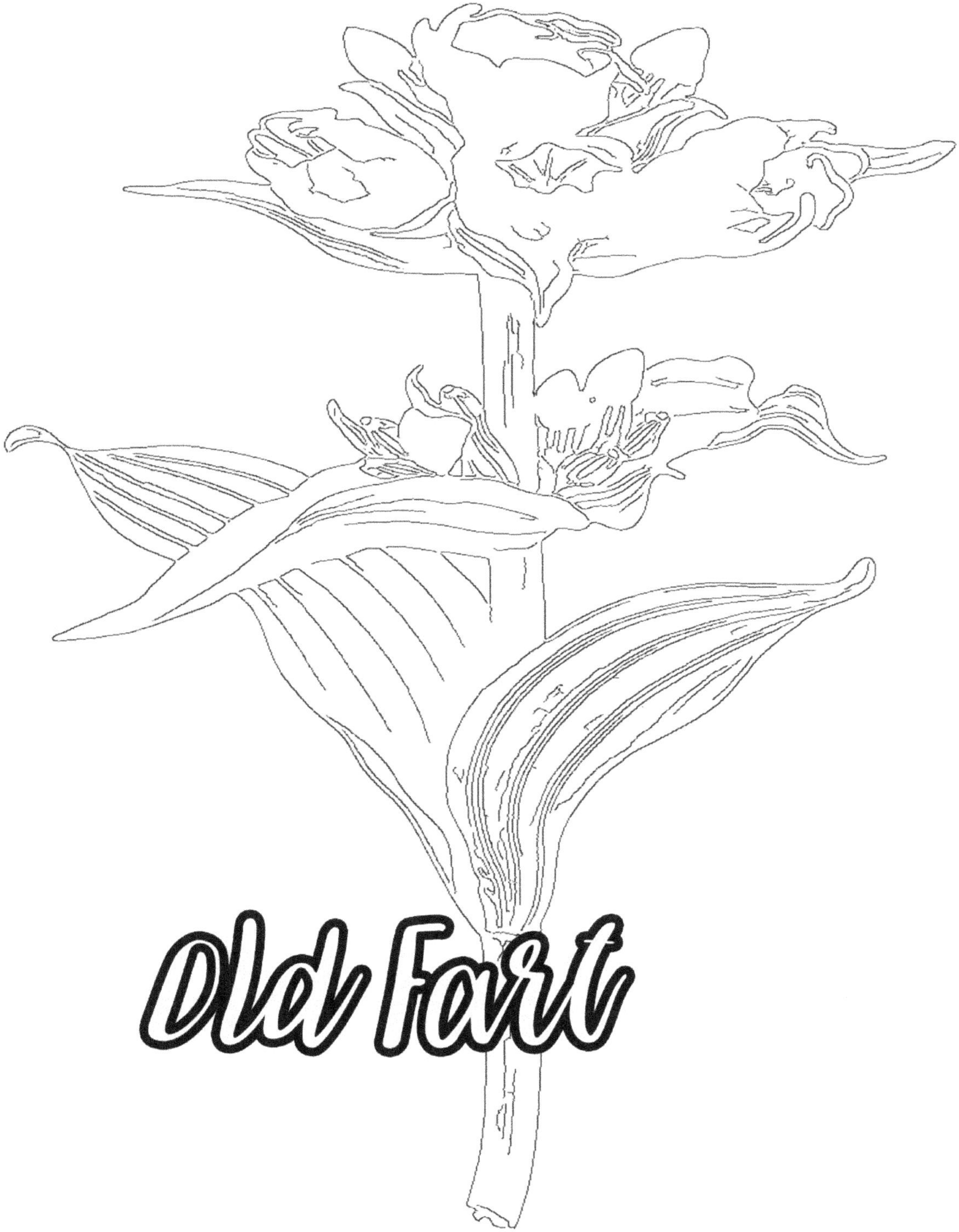
Old Fart

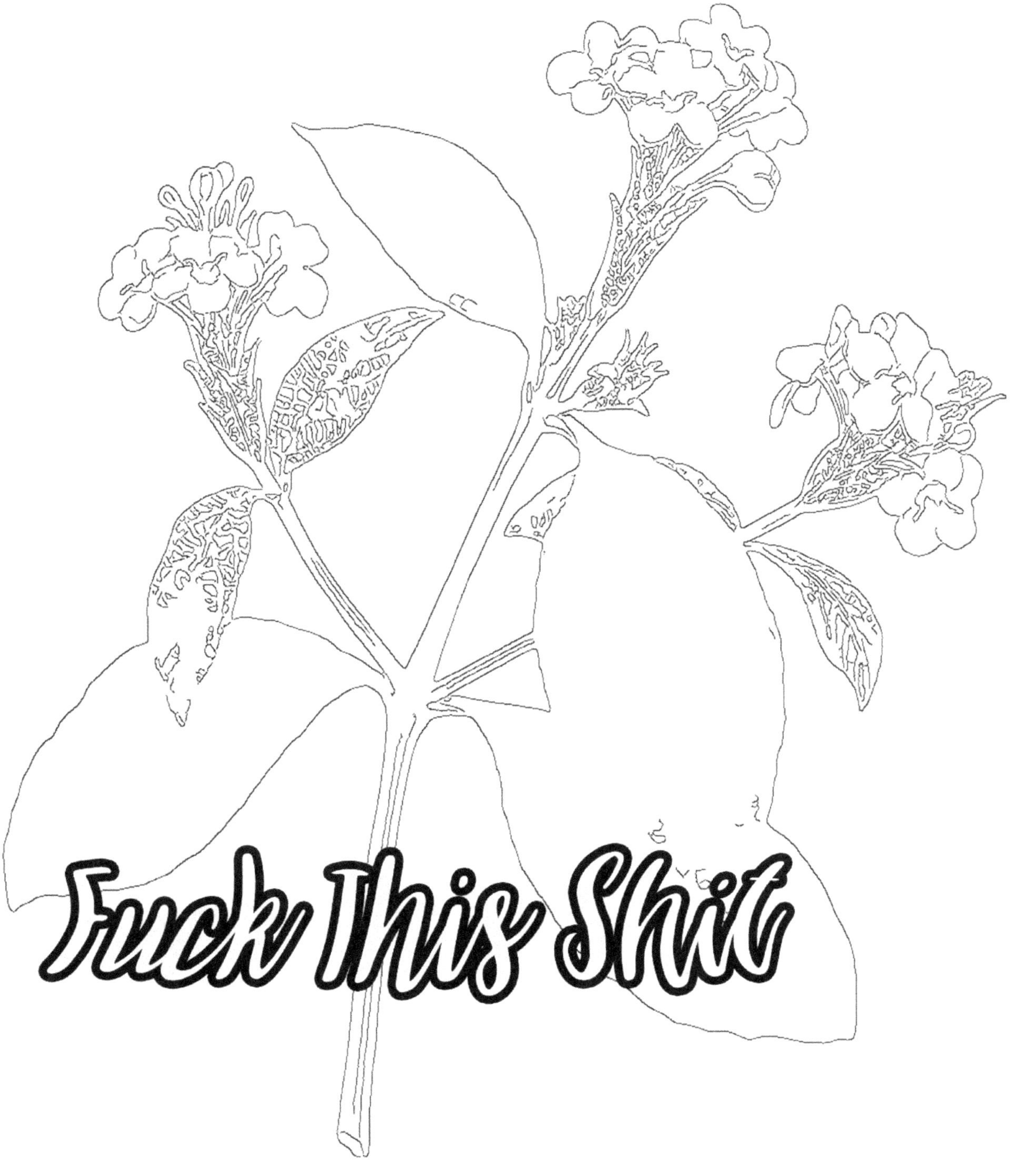
Fuck This Shit

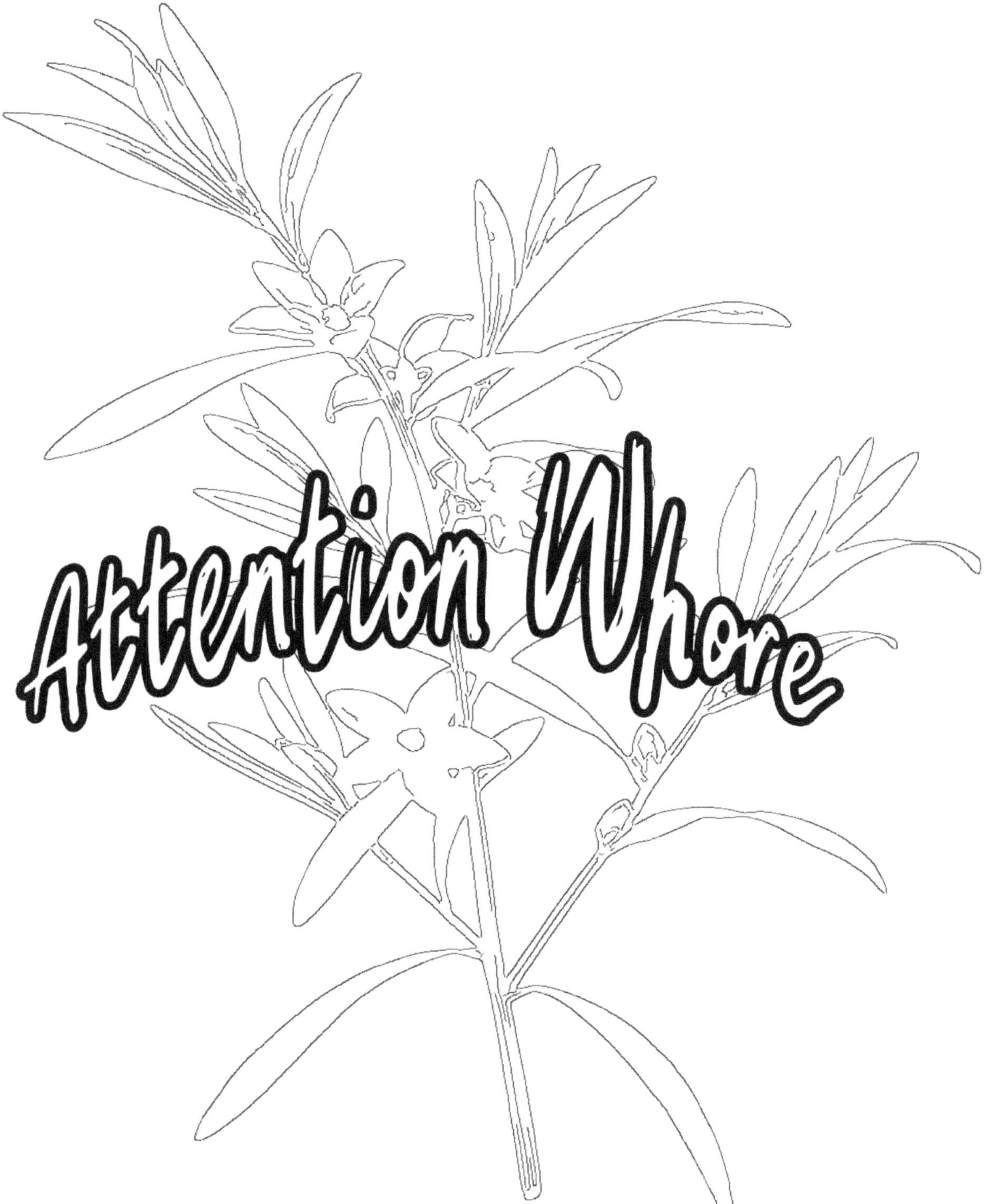
Attention Whore

Have a good day.

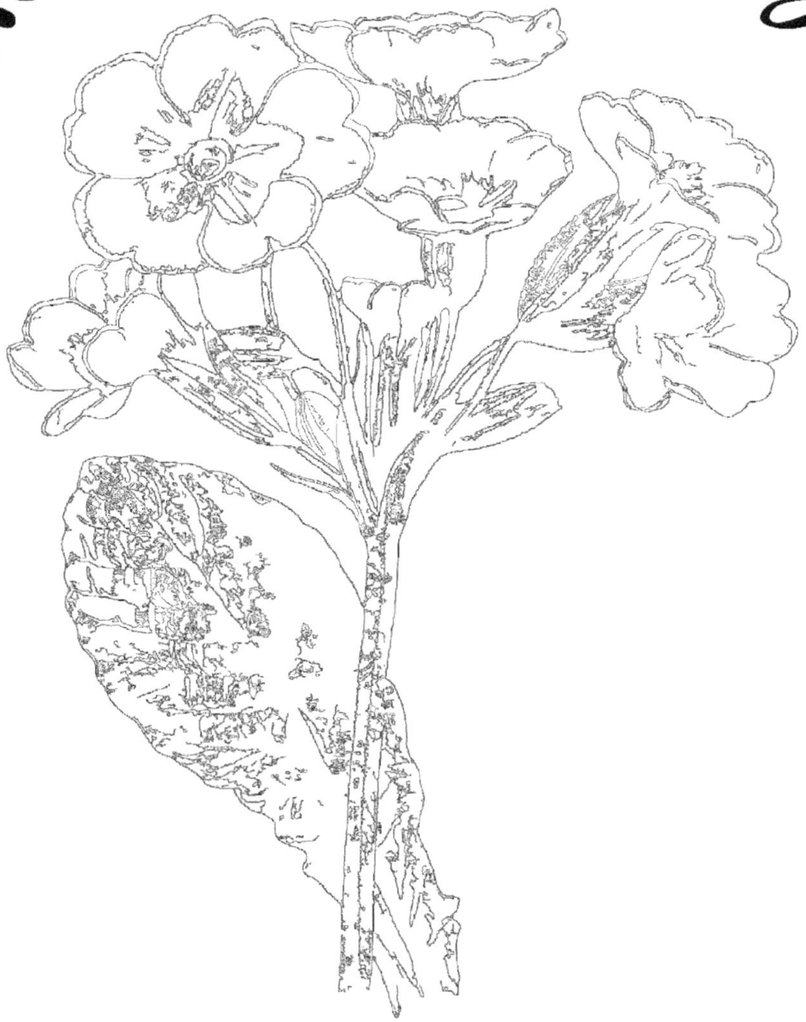

www.ingramcontent.com/pod-product-compliance
Lightning Source LLC
Chambersburg PA
CBHW081618220526
45468CB00010B/2938
9781983670213